KEWALO BLUES AND ECHOES

POEMS

KEWALO BLUES AND ECHOES

POEMS

GARY PAK

BLAZEVOX[BOOKS]
Buffalo, New York

Kewalo Blues and Echoes
by Gary Pak
Copyright © 2024

Published by BlazeVOX [books]

All rights reserved. No part of this book may be reproduced without
the publisher's written permission, except for brief quotations in reviews.

Printed in the United States of America

Interior design and typesetting by Geoffrey Gatza
Cover Art: Gavin Iwai

First Edition
ISBN: 978-1-60964-460-4
Library of Congress Control Number: 2023950171

BlazeVOX [books]
131 Euclid Ave
Kenmore, NY 14217
Editor@blazevox.org

publisher of weird little books

BlazeVOX [books]

blazevox.org

21 20 19 18 17 16 15 14 13 12 01 02 03 04 05 06 07 08 09 10 11

BlazeVOX

ACKNOWLEDGEMENTS AND THANKS

First and foremost, I want to thank my parents, Etta Chung Hee Young Pak and Francis Chin Chan Pak, and my grandparents, Lim Ok Soon, Young Eung Whan, Kim Sook Ahn and Pak Ho Byeong, for the obvious reasons why I am here and working in the realm of culture.

For the immediate purposes of this book, I want to acknowledge the following institutions: Department of English and The Center for Korean Studies, both at the University of Hawai'i at Mānoa; Ewha Womans [sic] University in Seoul, South Korea; and the Toji Cultural Foundation in Wonju, South Korea. There are many people to thank, and these individuals come immediately to mind: Boo Kyung-Sook; Kim Se-hee and Kim Na-yeong; Susan Schultz; Rob Wilson; and Wing Tek Lum.

And, of course, the best comes last. My deepest aloha to my wife and our children, their spouses, and our beautiful grandchildren.

TABLE OF CONTENTS

In the Memory of Joy Aulani Ahn and Gwen Epuni Kim

Kewalo Blues and Echoes

Poems

Ke-walo. Section 22 of Honolulu (map 6), basin (harbor), and surfing areas, one called Ke-walo (Diamond Head side of the channel) and another, Point Panic ('Ewa side). Outcasts (kauwā) intended for sacrifice were drowned here. Lit., the calling (as an echo).

From Mary Kawena Pukui, Samuel H Elbert and Esther T. Mookini. *Place Names of Hawaii*. Honolulu: University of Hawaii Press, 1974.

1

The tide is out tonight
And so the wind, the air
Drawn out past the break,
Residual of a hot summer.

Bruddah Kawika is lying
On his side facing the sea,
Bicycle standing next to him.
He is already dreaming
With the stars and the fish
Mating in the sea, this sea.

Old white-haired woman
Fishing on the wall, what will
This night bring? An endless
Spinning of your line?
A patient waiting out of
Time that holds
Nothing for you
Or him?

2

For Paul

Emerald walls of water line up
From one edge of horizon to the next.
Slow and methodical, they roll towards
        shore, splashed with white light
Sparkling on wind-whipped faces.
Converging on rocks like
        echoes of hushed thunder.

Minutes ago a hope of basic
        living was thrown
        against the wind
As if nothing is inevitable.

                Thunder collapses
                Reverberates
                On lava boulders.

3

There are sprinklings of heads
At one edge of the picture,
Surfers wait for sets to
Call their own.

How deep is this ocean? Does
it fly into the realm of air?

They study the wind
    and surface of the waters,
    size up the swelling set,
    size up each other, who
    is in the right position, who
May be lucky to catch the wave.
The others will wait
    for their chance
    to turn to the wind.

4

I always enjoy the sounds of sea
At this edge of night
I imagine stars rolling like
      breakfast before me,
and see them vanish in a dust of dawn.

If there is one fear I have, it is
Not the fear of death, but
The fear of witnessing time unchanged,
A stalling of all things decaying.
If this ever happens, then time
Will turn back, reverse itself.
Then where will we all go?

Perhaps the new age will be then
The old age and no age, and the yes,
Or light might reverse itself
And no light will be all light.

It would be something to see:
The waves unbroken
And returning
To the void.

5

Black crabs resurrect from cracks
In large boulders after washing
Of waves, a hundred eyes prodding
Over what the waters have cast
On these rocks, porous
And hard, volcanic renderings
That tell the story of a young land.

These black crabs live in a community
But they fight over scraps of food.
But there's a lot of food out there.
All this bickering and ranting
And rattling their shields and claws
And all of this nonsense that
Goes nowhere—every day,
        or every wave that comes—
All of this just keeps them
        as crabs.

6

It's Looney Tunes tonight.
It's in the echo of the night
That flies beyond the breakers
Of this long dawn.

People stealing, talking trash,
Acting like it's a full moon,
But it's not:
>   the moon is high near
>   the north star and
>   it's a half moon.

People should be only
Half crazy and not indecent
>   at all.

The fishermen should be hauling
In big leaps rather than
Suffering the wait.

Oh, it's Looney Tunes tonight.
The waves are breaking one way
And crashing in another.
Foam spreads on the
Face of the next wave.
Is it going in or out?

It's Looney Tunes, this blinking

Of colors telling me

It's time, to pack my pen

And ride off to the sanity

Of rubber-slipper land.

7

At Kewalo's
Ocean heals the spirit.
Its vastness pinpoints
A place for your soul.
Boat goes in, then out.
Air enters and exits

And gives wonder, direction
And caution for what comes
Today and tomorrow,
Yesterday.

Waves break and leave
No impression but dry
Into salt that toughens
Body, preserves your spirit
And passion.

8

My back is to the ocean.

From ground zero
A paper tiger shoots up
Into the hawaiian blue.
Some white pilot in the service
Of the almighty (who looks haole)
Would kill nameless people
In his name. How can an honest
Poor people struggle justly
Against a machine whose one part,
A wing, is worth a treasury that
Could feed an African nation
For a year?

Peace Man's back is turned to the ocean.
I pedal past him, again,
This time he is studying a newspaper,
Not strumming his weather-worn white Telecaster.
I wonder where he thinks he is
When he twangs a rusty chord.
Is it a hopeful sound?

haole: Hawaiian, white person

How many ears do you have, o sea?
I have but just two that take me
As far as where the red lights weep.
I am guilty that I cannot hear all
You tell me about the lines of
The sand floating on your face, about
The pipers singing rhapsodies on
Sweet wind blowing from day's edge,
About whirly waters colored sinfully
In beiges and rouges to the palates of air,
About the playing of children in the folds

       of green green seaweed pulling
        and pushing the currents of shame.

I am sorry I cannot hear all of
Your laments and accolades to the sun
And moon, and I know you don't care
Because you live the time
That you have and don't know how to
Mark the distance between the walk

       of the sun and the rhetoric
       of fluted sounds that grow ears.

10

The water is drawn out, far, exposing

Dead rocks. The fishermen are out,

What they are going for, who knows.

There's a hibachi firing and the sounds

Of two waves making love, and the universe

Seems to be about day and night, night

And day, and no in-betweens and no

Reflection and no joy of seeing

New things and new wonders, the joy of

Sound and sense, play and rest,

The crackling of charcoal and

Grilling of dried squid. So when

The red lights blink, and the green,

Whose sanctity are they applauding?

Not here, not there, but where?

Beauty is not in the sharp lines

Of absence. There is much

To see in the in-betweens

And the mixings thereafter.

We round the turn and go nowhere.

The map before us tells truths.

But the beacon rises in the east

And we don't know where it comes from.

Perhaps we are supposed to know,

And that's what makes it believable.

The sky rises to the colors of time

And yet we are told that simple

      desires are but wanton.

And we dribble our needs in this

      mire of nonsense.

Our worlds are narrow; we do

      not see more than what

      the horizon and its sounds tell.

We need to play the keys of

      the universe.

That is all. And

That is all.

12

'A'ama crab crawling over black rock,
Can you see me like I see you?

Push and pull of waves on rocks.
Rocks wearing away.

One thing no one can catch
Is a wave.

I no need know why
This windy salt air
Gives me peace.

The beauty of breaking water.
Disappearing the moment
            I see it.

'A'ama: Hawaiian, a black rock crab

13

What can I make of this night?

My eyes are blurry, squeaky to focus.

The sea has disappeared into darkness.

Moon plays off wind-blown

    waves like animated pixels.

I come to sing my song to watery

    rhythms but am flat.

The lights blinking off coast are

    trying my personal symbolism.

                 They fail.

The fishermen have turned into drunks.

My bicycle and pen are my

    only friends that can run

    with me in the toss of wind.

My only friends? Don't know if

The fish will bite, ever, in this

Windy turn.

What can I make of this night?

Where can I laugh?

Stay, crab, in your hole, that piko on

The black rock's top that now

You call home. Waves push on you and

Give sustenance but

When afternoon sun drops you'll be

Fair game for poachers of your soft flesh.

So river runs and runs over your home

And still you lie haunch in this mix

That has taken you into its porous colors.

How long will you last this way with

Your arms splayed in alert?

piko: Hawaiian lit., navel

15

Water in.

        Water out.

     Water in and out.

When does it end? The pleasuretube riders

Getting fluff with foam, then the seabirds

Shatting on splashes of wave.

In and out,

       and in.

              Until death do you part?

What did Van Gogh see in the stars

That night over a hundred years ago? Where

Did his vision take him, along the poles

Of lights, against the charm of heaven's odors

That kept him casting a feathery net on and on

Into the deep, dark blue-blue of it all?

And how far did he need to fine tune

The baton he used to nick the hard

Colors of trees, you know, the ones

Gone on and on bearing

Fruit of no comparison,

Implements of an artist's heavenly

Vision of what these lights might

Suggest to us born as mortals,

Sentenced to finding justification

Of awe and wonder

Silenced by the rise and fall of waves

Surrounded by desires and glances

Signed by external devices known only

By thinkers and generators of capital—

      Why can't we just see like Van Gogh?

I don't have the patience of a fisherman
Who instead of searching for the run lets
The run search for him. I don't have time
To watch black turn white, the fall of a tree,
A transformation of a quail, nor for the
Toll from a belfry. I just don't have the time.
I am impatient. I can't wait for the wind
To change a mountain, for the breeze
To touch my soul, for a response from
A jilted lover. I need to touch all
Forty continents by the third dawning.
I can't wait for the fish to bite.
I just can't wait for moments to freeze and punctuate
Themselves on this rhapsody of rhapsodies.
Just let the waves break. Let the
Fool eat his stories. Let the leery
Continue their jawing. Let the non-thinkers
Think they are thinking. Just leave me
Alone about all of this because

      I just can't wait.

18

There is uncertainty in this night,
The way the waves peel with no purpose,
The way buoy lights bend in the distance,
As if there is a careless feeling rendering
In this air that blows in strange streams.
I just can't figure it out, this feeling
This night, why the earth seems so
Uncaring, unforgiving, when simple
Friendships cannot pass the boundaries
Of humanity, when a homeless man holding
An umbrella warns about a vision of violence.
Why is there so much uncertainty?
I know why. It's because no one
Just gives a rip, no one just cares
About simple things like enjoying
This salty air, the blue of sea,
The wonder of stars, the simple
Love between best friends.

19

Situate two chickens in a ring and they will fight.

Let them run wild in a yard and they will live.

These chickens drag me into this

      madness they call "social justice."

It's not social justice, it's a way to

      make one's ego advantageous over another.

That's what it is.

A fair warning: Don't push me too much more.

My volcano will erupt, and I'll unleash

      a flood of magma, stones that are

      ballistic and will bury you.

Then what will you have to say?

Will you have something to say?

Or will you give up and be roasted,

      like a chicken

In Costco?

How I love the salt in this air!
And the sun warming my affair
With this wind that teases me,
Confronts me, but more so feeds me
With warm coolness. But it's
The salt in the air, baked on the
Flat black rocks, that nourishes
My lungs and skin, despite
Rough shadows of jets
Reminding me of tastelessness.
Why do I consider the lives of those
Who pester me, pester all,
Who force us to look
In fiction for the truth of our lives?

Such a joy, here, to sit on this rock
And write! Such a joy. As I look
Over the channel and see a millionaire's
Yacht with rich haoles basking in this
Paradise and yes, with Diamond Head
In the background. Such a joy!

Such a joy to see fishermen struggle
With time and the right bait to use.
Such a joy. To see surfers line up
For the next wave—who's the bull…now?
Who's counting?

Such a joy to sit here and not be
A part of this beautiful picture, with
The sonic booms of fighter jets letting us
All know who is the boss. Such a joy.

Such a joy to leave that messy corridor
With artificial turf and barf-flavored
Words finely tuned by book learning and
The right-college degrees. Such a joy.

Such a joy to sit here and see a smile

And really feel

    Joy.

22

Lonely star,
Are you my favorite thing
In this sea of glitter, this
Pushing and pulling of threads
Like meaningless words of a toothless sage?
Maybe I should ask the white-haired woman
Who sways her bait all night long:
Eh Lady, what is your favorite thing?
She will turn and give me
One stink eye and go back
To her bobbing lure. Perhaps she
Is waiting to catch her favorite
Thing?

I have a favorite person, and he is
Thousands of miles away, making
Me smile, and the chilly wind
Compells me to beg for warmth
And a golden blanket
As it whips and whorls
In the wildest of winters.

23

Here he is, the scooper of water,
Every day at this very spot with his
Net bought ages ago, patched several
Times with tsuji, dipping his scooper
In this pond of brackish water,
Scooping on and on, trying to catch
Not fish but the nature of water.

O water…
How royal and religious you are.
Everyone tries to capture your
Powers, your illusive face, that
Challenges everyone to the ends of time.
Did I say "ends"? Water, will you
Agree with me that time is a plural
And not a linear equation? I know

The scooper trying to find your
Secrets in the easiest way
Would possibly agree with me.

tsuji: Japanese, nylon fishing line

While the fisherman whips his line into
The wind and surfers maneuver for
Winter waves, a wedding takes place.
A young couple from Japan waits at a spot
That looks towards wonderful Diamond Head.
Eight thousand miles they have travelled,
With their small party—family? friends?—
Who will witness this wedding of whispers—
How long will it last? But imagine
The squeals of delight they might have had
When they saw the outline of that jagged
Old cinder cone. They will have their fun,
While the fisherman waits for a bonefish
While playing a game on his iPhone.

Time—old friend who calls anywhere
Home—tells another story when a
Shift in the wind, or mood, or flow of
Water changes the world of the known.
But believe in this: When laughter is
Wisdom, when flexibility is nonexistent,
When sweetness of suddenness and
Doing seems packed up and gone,
Believe this that Time will not give
You any sizing of the sun's growth,
Or the parsing of plants, nor will Time
Find a secret place where you can call
Home. Only you can manage what
Occurs in your space. Time will
Give you wrong answers and knock
Against your privileges that only
You can gratefully call your own.

I am hungry for words
That will take me to
Watery pleasure, that will
Slather me with foam of folly
That now has fallen over me—
Yes, slather—so I can feel how
Ridiculous this is all about.

Nothing matters except for
Purest of love that grows
Every day in the wrinkles
I nourish,
Line after line,
Page after page,
Wild images committing
Themselves to no structure,
Just blatant laughter basking
Out on the limb, soaking up
Resins of a good day, a very
Good day, this day,
This is.

27

Restless waverings, day in, day
Out, but today, working as I do
With small vision but work ethic
In place, I discover something new
That deals me great pleasure.

How happy I am, having
Worked this hard and a small
Gift comes to a page after
Empty ramblings.

How happy I am to take
This day and make it my own.

Leaves tossed about in the breeze
Of a sea storm. Browned by the sun
And mixed with trash of the passersby.
Who knows of your genealogy?

There is an order in the way they
Lie that no artist can ever
Conceive, no writer can ever
Describe, no cellist can ever
Contrive the air for, in this
Breeze that comes along, this way
And that, for as long as time
Has been sensing the rubbings
Of earth's fiery spices.

Hello, my friend, long time no see.

Thank you for greeting me with your

Salty hand, your breath heavy with

Limu and wana, like your cousins

I saw last week. It's been a long time

Since I felt your good charms—

I thought were gone, forever.

Every day people ask me how I'm

Doing, though they don't say

It right. Not the right tempo,

Not the right cadence,

Just not the right color of water.

Yes, the color of your water is

Just right. Thank you,

My friend, for the color of your water.

limu: Hawaiian, seaweed

wana: Hawaiian, sea urchin

Waves roll in ceaselessly,

On and on, each different than the other,

Tempered by the elements of nature—

Chemistry, weather, salinity,

Coral formations—and

The topography of the coast's bottom.

Yes, they change in magnitude

And shape over a large journey

In time

       Change is good.

I want to be a wave,

    always rolling

    omniscient

    cool

Changing.

The front one is tall and lean and

Has no imperfections. No one climbs it

As, if one does, one would climb ten feet

Then fall to the sun-hardened ground.

It rises with a clean, straight line

To the sky. The other, behind,

Is taller but it's not straight,

Has bent this way and that as it grew

To the lower clouds. Its skin is scarred

With the digging of cleats

Of a climber who perhaps once found

The water of its fruit refreshing.

Its skin has many imperfections.

If I am to choose beauty

Between the two

my choice is the one

Not afraid to show its faults.

Waiting

For breaking waves

And the incandescent shimmer

Of water rising and falling,

On the complexion of no-fault

And dimpled and porous rock,

Scented with cat dung.

Waiting

For what?

Buy a bottle of toothpaste, the

One that operates off the fire engine's siren,

You know, the one that

Concocts ideas as good as anyone

But who can't put

Paint on canvas.

Like the rainbow in the valley.

33

Quiet

Now

When ocean melds to evening,

When bricks of the outdoor shower are blackened wet,

When the fisherman, with downcast eyes,

     dons his hat and sets up his gear,

Casting into an empty sky.

The limestones are cut right,

Set into a wall, and the tides

Punch the wall while a squatter

Packs his cigarette. But

It's quiet here

And sounds reverberate into melodies

And the sky—yes, the sky—

Becomes a blanket for

Dreams.

Seaweed! What a wonderful life you have,
Anchored to a rock, rolling with the waves,
Being free to form a fine romance with the elements,
Touching the sandy bottom then pluming up
To the star-dazzled surface of the waters
That are always nourishing, always striking
With soft palates of recognition.

Oh seaweed!
How admirably you dance
Between the claws of crab, through
The windpipe of the moray, by the hour
And on the hour of the swelling moon.

Seaweed! How your salty sweet taste
Smacks the lips of fishermen who
Have not learned to dream yet
To the dance of dawn's dampening sun.

35

Hard salty wind tries to pull
The whiskers from my face. My pen
Wobbles while I write. My shorts balloon
Into pantaloons. And the waves look
Rushed, panting in their effort to pass time.

I know for a fact that: once in
The forest a demon will look longer
Than it should. That: my eyes
Can't focus when I see two things
Of beauty at the same time. That:
Water can nourish and kill you,
And cleanse you from the most
Disagreeable odors of sleeping
Landlords. That: How much you might
Satisfy your urge, you will never
Satisfy it. That: It is impossible
To not be changed by a single squeeze
Of sunlight.

This night plays funny music
At times sprinkling wet motes
On my cheeks as if taunting me with
Elevated surprise. Yes, this night
Plays with me, laughs at me, teases me,
Tells me why don't you play
Your favorite tune, why not sing
It aloud and wickedly instead of letting it
Echo on and on in your head,
Warping your mind with its
Mad musicality. But I tell back:
Hey, I like warp. I like echo.
I like melody.
And I like sing it on and on
Even if you tease me
With your raspy voice begging me
To keel over and
Say my music is yours.

There cannot be a better place than

Here, today, under this windy sun, in

This sweating body that has been satisfied by

A nourishing lunch and the company of a good friend,

My 27-speed mountain bike, fabricated in

China, under the watchful eyes of

Pseudo Marxists who claim

Ten Modernizations are better than

Ten Relationships among people.

No, there is nothing that can substitute

This better place and feeling. Here, I

Can listen to the pleasing and uncluttered

Laughter and banter of the waves, the

Roll of the breezes, and the dappling

Of rain as I sit on this rock,

Pen in hand, notebook in other, and

Write a poem to this bliss.

...we can dream good dreams again.

Hone Tūwhare

Let us dream good dreams again,

You and I,

As we raise our words of love

With the risk of being overthrown,

When we share laughter and food

   among friends with the joy of afternoon,

While we sing our songs of wonder

   colored in the reveries of a rainbow.

When we hold our hands,

   with heads bent together,

   our hair turning gray,

   and we smile at the

   dreams that were lost

And the dreams that we live

Now—

   Let us dream good dreams again.

It is the idiot that steps on a box

And declares everything is

Insignificant.

Really? Insignificant?

How much fury of sound does one

Have to pursue before the insignificance

Turns to significance? Like those

Nodding heads waiting for waves

To come his or her way. Is this

A size of the insignificant?

Or do we need to hold a gun and

Point in an honest direction before

The insignificance becomes signified?

    Waves ebb and flow,

    Wandering on and on

    Like pixels on a screen.

When in the beginning do we
Know the end? When the clouds
Turn to chalk? When the drizzle
Feels like rain? The disposing
Of waves is everywhere,
But now the sun seems like
The moon, and the stars are
But droplets on the celebration
Of the night. The pen becomes
A hindrance to thought.

But now I need the
Shelter of a waterproof
Jacket, and the pedals
Are my freedom.

41

Waiting in line for nearly half of an hour

To purchase a discounted pair of sunglasses

To protect my eyes from the hot Hawaiian sun.

I guess it was worth it. So now I can

Toss out my new-old pair that broke

At the plastic temple. How long will this

Pair last before it too will be obsolete,

One small crack in the frame, making it

Useless, which

Will prompt me

To return to this

Bargain store and stand in line

To buy another plastic gadget

That will one day breakdown

And fuck up this

Dying world?

How happy this bride from Japan looks

With the background of a peaceful sea.

And look at all of these haole photographers

With their cannon-like cameras pointing

For that protracted perfect wave!

Waves come in

Waves go out

Whitewater all around

Is this the refuge I seek from

Headless chickens complaining

As they scratch dirt for worms?

In Betweens looks nice. It calls me

Back thirty years plus, those days

With no emails, no headaches, no cell phones,

Just sunburns and laughter and dreams
Of love.

In Betweens: name of a surfing spot off the coast of Honolulu

43

I wonder if I could write a poem
That would talk to the waves about
The wind and her problem, or
The grief about identity and how
Others—those careerists—want me
To believe what mine is.

Oh sea spray! You are refreshing
Like malted water, like the dash
That bursts on the off-shore breeze,
A mat of wondrous pubic hair on my face.

Now, identify that.

It doesn't matter how one does it;
It just matters that one is happy,
And one is lucky, perhaps extremely,
To share this happiness with
Someone who can thread the needle,
Who can talk about visions,
Who can share in a day or two a table
Of reminisces and laughter about
a world so rounded and so squarish,
a universe so clean and denatured
That they are startling and crisp
And colorful to me
And you.

45

Black rock, different shades
Of black, one flat rock
With a bowl to collect water,
Now encrusted with salt crystals.

Two sets of fishers, both talking
Into the wind that brings me
Bright conversation that hides
The other. But I hear too

The rascal jeers of children's joy
And laughter and the rattling
Of training wheels on brick. Oh, children,
Please leave the cakes of salt alone.

The wait of the fisherman is but

A championship at the end of time. Behind

Dark glasses coated with anti-reflective film,

He adjusts the gradations of sun and mood

Of clouds, sometimes taking hours,

Sometimes days and weeks, sometimes

Always. And when there is a nibble

In these overfished waters, does he

Find pleasure or does he feel

Time is checking on

To infinite fields where verse

Becomes play, where water

Moves on and out into rushing

Folds to unearth stones from

Material connections and pleasures?

Just you and me, sea. I will take

You to the ends of your dappled horizon.

No, I take that back: until my arms

Tire from paddling this board. But

It's so peaceful out here, just you

And me, wondering with no meaning

At our thoughts, creating this warm

Mood, this happy mood, that is chilled

By off-shore breezes that do

Not want to give up on

You and me, sea. I don't know why

I have never done this before,

Share this horizon with you, sea,

Or rather, acknowledge your sharing

Of this beauty with me, sea,

My comparison in my earlier years,

My companion when I feel or can see no more.

Waikīkī! O Waikīkī!

Why do people flock to crowd

Your shores? To buy your aloha tokens?

To be under Lēʻahi's visage? To

Walk your lovely sands and wade in

Your tropical waters and to be inspired

To write meaningless poems of

People fucking you inside and out?

Take that scruffy haole who wears

The trousers of a tourist and yells

Upward at the hotel balconies about

The tragedy in his life: "How can a

Tenured MIT professor be terminated?!"

O Waikīkī! I've given up on you.

Well, I have for most of my life.

I wish I could be able to help you

But why should I help something

That was already fallen and selfishly

Wants to take everyone else, too?

Lēʻahi: Hawaiian, original name for Diamond Head

Once again I come to this spot where
Waves crush rock and leap towards me.
My shoes are soaked in the first lunge,
As if a wave says, who you? Filmy limu
Holds on to black rocks. These waves
Can touch them but not shake them free
From their roots in rocks' pores.
I like to think I am like limu,
Going with the flow, flexible, nutritious
And deeply taken into the nature of
These ways. But perhaps I'm more like
Those bobbing heads over that reef
Across the channel, watching and waiting
For a swell that will make them sway.

50

Loose Rock

Wind blows sea spray in my face.
The taste of salt. The taste of limu.
This rock gives me an unsteady step to
The water's edge, but there's just
A little play and not enough to lose
My step. Just need to learn how to
Play with these loose rocks that run
The course of the trail. Sometimes
They let you fall and let you pick
Yourself up again. Sometimes
They make you wonder why all
These rocks on this path are not
Wet and lovely like this one.

Leaves drifting on wild water,
Going this way and that, and no where.
How can they fight the force of foam?
Or thunder of the roll that knows no end?
Yet they remain, gelled together
In a line that seems to taunt
The boil of elements, picking up
Bits and pieces and other mysteries.
One wonders if this is a synecdoche
Of a larger overflow, an anemic venturing
Of bloodless spirits who somehow have
Come to understand the sentiment
That keeps them afloat and pondering.

Deep light, tell me your song.

Is it sounding off these rocks or

Is it traveling across the limu-crested

Reef? I'm trying to hear your colors

But I'm having a hard time feeling the odors

Of this fresh vapor you're jettisoning

Towards me. Why do you make this process

So hard? Why can't you be simple

Like the swan dancing off a reflection

Or like a game of marbles among school boys?

Why make this business difficult? All I want

Is to feel your suspicions

About the rise and fall of the sun,

And in what directions the birds fly.

A leviathan waits

To be born,

To be resurrected,

Among ourselves, just waiting

To rise from our rehearsals

With the gods of memory,

Asleep now but ready when the time

Erupts like a full moon

Over a plain of smiling devils

Around the

Or to be imagined

    hastening

Fireplace of our

Wandering blood and aroused eyes,

With which we have played

Among our many songs.

Nothing to say today. Nothing. Not even

A mind's picture to sow a stimulated fool.

Not a hunger for a breeze, or a desire

For a fleeing yellow tang. Just nothing.

Nothing. A smile lasting for a few seconds.

At least this pen works. My way to this

Rocky seat was pleasant. Got no real

Complaints. Just ideas to oppress the mind,

This history to bleed a soul, this water

That brings me more thirst and a desire

For the wantonness of a simple

Fashion and a simple hold on a thought—

Just a thought—of what is it like to hold

On to a rhapsody that drifts here from a muse.

55

Homeless

The theme is everywhere, it seems, and
Decorates the trees that we buy, then discard
For mulch. Why even think the word "home"?
Makes people sad, makes people desperate, makes
The lion turn into a puppy dog or a pile of shit.
Why do you tell me to go home when
I don't have a home? I'm homeless. Don't
You know the song that tells about
A joy to blow a tune on a flute
From a willow tree? Do you claim this is but
An abstract thought, nothing at all?
Stop telling me this nonsense, or don't
Try to understand me—I don't like you
And will never like you because you are
Living on my home.

The window to the wind comes once in

A lifetime—actually, it has always been here.

It's just we don't know how to smell it,

Or we just don't know how it smells.

That's the tragedy of it all—we can spend

An ancient's time and not even know it's here.

To give us a flavor to feel, that would make

All this good turn bad, and turn good back again. But

Here's the problem: The window or windows

Are owned by descendants royale

And otherwise of the original inquisition. But

We know they exist: We've many dreams of them

And know they are real. First step: Let's stop

Waiting or the windows will fall into the waves.

Weaving in and out of the fingers of coral, between

Shreds of seaweed, balanced by its anchor on a rock,

And the surge of the sea, the yellow tang runs

Along beneath the froth, pecking here and there,

All day long for nourishment of algae, that gives

Them energy and growth to survive another day.

Another day! But they know nothing of Monday,

Or Saturday or Wednesday. They do feel

Thickening of water that makes their fins

Flail or fly or flutter, or float above it all.

They don't know death or a daily life

Or a talking stone narrating stories

Of wonder and fear and storms of superstition.

They know nothing. They just roll with the waves,

Swim among the shapes of shadows, then die.

Like ripples raging to shore, so are words
Foaming from the tips of tongues, like
Rabid sprays of a mad dog. Do they have
A center to call a definition? Do they have
A certainty to claim?
They seem aware of the rapidity
Of surcharges and the other
Amenities that publicity offers,
But how can they be so sure and so calm?
Even great ones do not stake hold to the recipe
Of the perfect word, the perfect thought.
The fact they continue to write
Is but proof of their inadequacies.

59

Proud moment shows itself like
An old dried scab, only it doesn't have
The color of distaste that rides
On the crest of an overcharged moon.
Ahead the distant lights might give
Some kind of reservation that turns
The rise of the swollen sun, and
Mounts on the dog-less days of dawn.
How many can you count, and offer,
Psalms of love, then parables of
Destruction and disease? How long
Do the sons and daughters of night
Need to nurture feelings of loss
Before expressing the comfort of light?

How things can reverse themselves in the sway
Of the sailing sun. The saltiness of sardines
Becomes a wonder to the everyday, a slant
Of what is what. And the surprise to hear
The corrected name is not one of land's calling
But one stamped on a dead can.
Oh torrid seas that break on these shores!
Can you for once give me a justified time
Of your spawning? How about giving
Answers to hints that I have heard
From the moment vows have been made?
There is no telling of the intensity of this sun.
The moon is ready to replace her worth
And to forget the fading years filled with lies.

Black boat slants to the horizon, between

Red and green buoys, while waves

Are enhanced by the keel's cut against the norm.

Yes, things can be that simple, not easy,

But simple. Perhaps the most simple ways are

The hardest. But like that boat heading

To its path known, can't the path be

Unknown and simple, too? Play with birds

And the songs will come. Sight the horizon

And the canvas will fill with colors

Of dawn and the sounds of dusk.

Run with the wind and stories will rise

From the gravel that one crushes

Daily and takes for granted, now,

With the magic of image, illusion and pun.

Fisherman claims his dinner

With a mouth of broken teeth.

He is dark like the emptiness of night,

Grins and points at blue-green schools

Of halulu under cockle shell of ocean.

Outside sets are coming in, bashing

Black rock with furious foam, eating

Deep into the cracks where 'a'ama crabs

Deflate in the syrupy swells.

Now cries of surfers lament

The here-and-gone-now blue wall.

Further out, towards the mountains,

The wail of an ambulance's siren

Fades into the swarthiness of the avenue.

Halulu: Hawaiian, baby Hawaiian mackerel

We turn to the sky when the winds bring us

The salt of the seas, and we study the stars as

If they will give inspiration. How loud they

Shine, we may claim, but these are but covers

To hide our ignorance. But sometimes beliefs

Droop like sagging lines of a fish-less season,

When the boughs of unwatered trees have

Their last gasp of wonder at the plight

Of gaping mouths standing

On end of each other as they reach

In some despairing way to grasp

Wisdom from the planets,

For any understanding that

Will never—never—be theirs to own.

Figuracion—can you tell me the boy you imagined

In the tall piledriver you watched when you

Took garbage from the haole boat club

To bins next to the brackish waters?

Why do you smile so boyishly? Why does your hair

Glean like a lost child, taking my mind to pastures,

Forests, deep mountains past outskirts

Of your ancestral village? Why does your simple smile

Make me lament, make me wish you can taste

The rich flavors that can make your smile

Complex and empty and yet lustful

For long desires and foolish appendages

Never in a lifetime you'll be able to

Amply dream

For another chance?

Bamboo, bending in wind, your leaves reach out

For a song. What's wrong with the song you already have?

Bugs try to infest your roots but with no success.

And sometimes the air pushes you hard, making you

Rattle against your tribe, but you always stay,

Rooted in your ground despite everything

That tries to prevent your straight growth.

Ah, yes, you are still growing strong and long,

Your limb muscled with green fiber that brings

Bounce to your bend, play in your laughter,

You know, the one I hear when hard wind

Roars from the mountain and forces

To your earth and heaven, threatens death,

Then disappears, swallowed by the sun.

Language is cruel. Makes me think I am going

Crazy. For example, the blue I see now is not

The blue I see tomorrow. But the blue I

See tomorrow is the same blue I see in today's water.

But all changes when the sun hides behind the clouds.

Or is it the clouds hiding the sun? Or…why is

Either "hiding"? Does a cloud or sun have a will

Such they will hide now like a stupid human

Who wants the entire universe to speak his

Or her language? And now the rain

From the valley comes down—but does it

Really "come down"? And "down"? And

Is it really called "rain"?

Once again yesterday follows me on my favorite air

And the photographer takes artsy pictures of flowers

Rather than weeds. Why can't I, like the eternal fisherman,

Cast out demons into the almighty forgetful sea?

Here, the waves will pulverize, and out there

They will be torn apart with frisky currents,

And all I do is sit on this sun-warmed rock

And complain to hell and beyond, this hell that

I do not believe in and yet seem to fall prey to.

Oh sea that has turned the color of earth,

Plead my case to the powers that slide deep

And rise high to wide workings of chastity.

Tell my yesterdays, for me, to leave me

Alone and love me only for my muse and testes.

68

Not sure how long those rocks will last

Signaling the reach of treacherous shallow waters.

But at least they are now beacon

Warnings of random renderings of nature.

They look strong to last a hurricane or two,

Perhaps more, though one day they will dissolve

Into the sea like everything else in the world.

But at least they will give fair warnings

Of what may come and what may harm.

There are things in this world that cannot hold

Ground to plastic warnings like these. For example,

How can you warn time or love to dispel truly

Myths that substantiate barebone understandings?

You three rocks, gray, wind-worn and sea-splashed,

Algae-crusted, you three have always given

Trusted warnings about waves to come.

Rough sea today. No surfers are out

In this mush. And that's odd. Aren't there

Surfers of all kinds, even some who would

Joy these takes with shapeless froth?

Yes, the sea is with an interesting mood today.

I wish I could capture this indifference

In a color on canvas, a mixing of aquamarine,

Slate and nonchalance to the tidal modes

Of one watching it with concern and prompt.

Yes, one color can be divided into many,

Each shade, each nuance a name of its own,

Each with its own suspicion, with its own

Carelessness, in this wide venue of sea,

Salt, froth, air, motion and song.

Only here near the sea we,
Stripped of our accoutrements,
Come close to a sunrise that
Promises beauty. Only here near
The heart of the land, where land
Meets original waters, do we
Find peace, rhapsody, that
Dares a cat to dance, that compels
Words to lie, to right the right
And the left of our existence
In the even moving turmoil
Of muck, of pleasantries, of
A time when dreams finally
Can be made good and wondrous.
Only here near the sea.

71

It's come around, again, another spiral,
Whether it's good or bad no one knows.
The fisherman takes another cast, takes
Another song, another hook or lure lost
To the whims of sea. The paddler dips
Another stroke in the current, the surface
Of ocean so peaceful, so calm, so peaceful.
I write another verse after many others, how
Many more will come I don't know, but
I am always telling myself to not think
About dead-end thoughts, though
Always I fail to take my own advice,
Because there'll always be another chance,
This, I am certain.

Warrior/Lover

I need to be a warrior and minister of peace
At the same time, to sermon the fires for
Justice and slay the laments of love.
We need to scope the inner wrath that
Bleeds with uncanny wonder and lust
And ram forth the plans of destruction and
Destination with wanton play of the powers
That be. We need to be both and all at the same
Time, at one time the other stronger than
The other, but never separate, never isolated from
Each other, never to be swayed either way
By a crazy sun-rashed woman-child growling
Cries and shoving a dead stick fish back
To the impermanent sea, waves washing ashore.

73

Shall we play this endgame
Where stars should shine but don't?
When anxiety challenges time but
The hussle is always a motion of
Nothingness? Where colors of blossoms
Are but lures to the senses, pointing
To a direction and to nowhere, stuffing
Our minds with the goods of beauty
And the aromas of temptation that
Make the heart fonder and palpate
For no good fucking reason?
Shall we play this endgame and
Wager the stakes that will make us
Sleep another night in the matrix?
Shall we play, or invent another game?

Just dots on the ocean,
Bobbing here and there over the currents
And rifts that take them this way or that,
Forward or backward, perhaps even under
To the glories be told, and all waiting for that
Wonderful rush that may give them a push
To some kin of tonal rectitude, some kind
Of out-posting of the mind, rapturous, monoaural
And deadly. Outside the plot begins, at high noon,
And inside the preachers deal their whispers
And other sorts of tragedies, and beyond all that
Comes along a puppy dog so friendly,
So unaware of sadness and despair,
But it too is a walking tragedy,
Waiting for that outside set.

Softly, softly the sun will fade, and the

Fisherman will offer his last dream to some

Translucent wish. At the bottom of this maybe

The absurdity of it all: a compact between

Saint and hermit crab—you know the one,

The one that hinders the progress of the demigod

By taking away the source of the torch. But

Somehow despite the horror of it all is

The pendulum that swings, not perpetually,

But still swings along that song of the sea,

That song that smells of crab offal and

Human urine that rises from ancient

Rocks I now sit on and gestate,

And the melody is abstract, warm and wanton.

Gentle rain, engage me with your rhythm,

That run of longing and sweetness that

Touches my quietness like fingertips on my chest.

How your fluids distend any measurement of time.

Gentle rain, you remind me of luscious hilltops

When, overlooking that roll of waves, the sky seems

A play for painters and poets of sand.

And gentle rain, weathering the raves of old,

How do you keep to your steadfast sad song

That brings a slower pacing to my thoughts,

That does not resolve but renders on and on

The flossing of soft images and random dreams

So that what's left are moments when

Love, loss and sadness fruit but more rain?

It's a Sunday at the park. Meat is grilling
And the children are laughing and the fish, maybe,
Are squirming in the narrow cracks of coral
Watching this madness. And couples are
Walking and I'm biking on my Giant and
It's such a sweet time, under this warm sun,
And I'm wondering how long will this all last.
Well, the red buoy's out, in its spot as always,
Anchored to the side of the passage in and so
The green one that spits a light at night;
And the waves, well, the waves, they seem
Okay. With an onshore wind, it's mushy,
But okay for young seals out playing.
And again I wonder, how long, how long will
This last before the sun stops showing up on time?

The rain has come, gone, and people have left
The park. This is the best time, I think, to be
Wet from the drizzle and sensing
All around this solitude, and not in a bad way.
I like this, to be with one's thoughts and
Not be bothered by someone's stupid jokes
Or supposedly slips of tongue. I should title
This, "The Solitude of Rain." No, I won't,
Why should I broadcast to anyone about
My joy to write in a rain-dappled book?
I am selfish. I want this solitude to be
Mine only. I don't want anyone to know
This pleasant solitude, this peace of soul.
I will keep this only to myself, to me, to I, to mine.

When waves break on shore,
We start our count of the numbers:
The width, the height, the volume that may
Contain an oasis for our
Journey to this known world. But, too,
We may find these calibrations confining,
Unabling us to see beyond the fourth wall,
Untransforming our wastrel thoughts into
The decimals of the unknown, of the
Finite lapping in this rampant hierarchical
Universe. Oh, but what joy it is, to just
Regard these waves just as they are,
As markers of time. Let's not
Brood on these self-imposed hardships
And rather expend the points of our total joy.

Words, words, the magical chute,

The more you use, the more it's moot.

And when the air is designed with knots

Perhaps it's time to end this suit.

But most of the time this doesn't happen

And words become dragons or daggers that

Relinquish power, like overthrowing

Dynasties and hauling in mountains like breasts

So pendulous that gravity will not work.

But words, words, yes, that magical fruit,

That one can hoot and one can too toot.

Make no mistake the dragon in the gas

That can make the world, the counterpoint

So untouchable, so gamely, so alluring to boot.

This is free—to be able to speak to the sky,

To taste the wind that comes a hundred miles away,

To smell the tension in the waves as they argue

With rocks and crabs. But don't they get along?

And among the clouds of unsmiling birds

There's a couple in white kissing to the rhythm

Of a photographer snapping, snapping,

An offering to the keepers of light. Oh!

The mighty splash that misses my pen

But touches my eyes! Oh, how

The wonders of sound punctuate

Sand and weed of the seas! Oh!

How my senses rise above like a balloon

On a hot sea and makes

Abandonment of the watch pure.

Ilokano Man

Tell your story, that's what you need to do.
Tell your story so your children and
Your grandchildren can know the humiliation
You had being called "boy" (no capital) by
One fifteen-year old haole Boy telling you
To get him one glass of water so he can
Feed his fucking fish. Tell your story,
Manong, about how you had to laugh
At dah fucking DeLima jokes cause the fat
Haole boys and girls were laughing too—you didn't want
Them to feel bad, no? Yeah, writing is hard,
Especially when you are not allowed to hold
A pencil to voice your creating thoughts.
But tell your story, Ilokano Man, so we
Can know the story of yours and live
To destroy the boy.

Ilokano: a person from Ilocos Norte, a province in the Phillipines
Manong: Ilokano, man
DeLima: a Local comedian

Soft, young, firm, why do the minutes

Turn to years? The tides go full, and now

The energy of the ocean has made all colors pastel-like.

Why do these feelings—these yearnings—make rise

To thoughts of raw laughter, fresh wantonness,

And futureless reckonings of the day-by-day?

Ah, youth! There was a time when the venerable,

Seasoned, mature were sought after like

Ripe fruits. Why not now and have it all?

Serpentine laughter is not desired, nor the workings

Of a juicy domain. What is wanted, desired,

Is the readiness to see the journey as it is

In this daylight and under the eyes of the moon.

None of this searching is required, just the the.

It's that nasty smell from the ocean again, coming

Back in on this hard onshore wind, bringing back

The smell that was taken out, to ferment among

The weeds and play of the stars among the sharks,

But now returning to tell us land people

How bad the land has become, overrun by

White invaders who hoist sails as

Toasts to their paradise regained,

A rationale to fucking up the ʻāina.

No, don't tell me how a species is endangered, nor

How the air is polluted—stop farting against

The wind. Stop telling me about

"Wholesome" and "Organic" and "This is cool"

When your presence has made it a hell for everyone.

ʻāina: Hawaiian, land.

The taste of the sea is a bouquet of pīkake.

Yes, those peacocks fly to the south.

(Or do they?) And behind that frame of glass

Towers insensate eyes can never blink and

And yet they prosper while the weather is in

A send mode. (How can that be?) When this

Reality is published, how many flowers from

This nasty nest will fight the flourish of

Boredom and regenerate to a kind of swarthiness?

The ships of empty passions await their belated

Importance by passengers who signify nothing

But themselves. Let them take bestial awards

That they bestow on themselves. Let them seethe

In pleasures that mean nothing. When they

Leave, it will make the air cleaner to the touch.

pīkake: Hawaiian, lit., pheasant. Name of the Hawaiian jasmine

flower.

Wind blowing west—very strong. I guess
I should be happy I'm riding in
Her direction, no? So many times I've ridden
Against her and now I'll let her carry me.
But this is okay, to ride with the wind.
Nothing elementary wrong with this, unless
One doesn't know where one's going, or
One does know what one's about but
Takes this ride and hides knowing
That others are blindly persuaded.
You can call this jumping on the bandwagon.
But as this poem is about riding the wind,
It's cool to know there are some
Who go against the wind when it tries
To destroy tomorrow's good visions.

87

The camera is but a lens
To the world that is
Focused on a few items.
In other words,
It's an exercise
On limitation.
So we live
In limitations,
And what we try to do
Is stretch the possibilities
Of these limitations
To make them seem
There are other venues
To pursue.
But the point is:
We have limitations,
So let's just explore them
As fully as possible.

How do we remake the stars that have already
Died when we become aware of their existence?
Is it possible to remake them, or have the errors
Transverse themselves into nothingness?

허감부   허감부   허감부

As if chanting of this word will bring an item!
But the question to remake one's self is
A challenge to be washed about until
The fabric is fragmented into simple parts.
The song of the dead ship at the bottom
Of the sea still resonates in ears of the hunted
And with quiet desperation. The transference
Of this energy is but a flimsy excuse for
The shaping of a word powerful and masterful.

허감부: Korean, nothingness. [pronounced 'heo-gam-bu']

The wait of the fisherman is better than

The search of the photographer for that shot

That will make herself memorialized.

Yes, the wait of the fisherman is lower-cased,

Not infatuated with its own self-proclamatory

Importance, yes, not like the wonder of the poet

Sitting on a rock expecting for a moment of ommm

To perch on his shoulders and shout in his ear.

The wait of the fisherman is the wait for

A precise touch of the wedge between time and

The fullness and fall of water, when the quickness

Of a dart offers him a snap of resistance

He can use to reach and take this offering

For his table and extend his memory of how

Tasty that fish was in the moment new and now.

The pages have crusted together from yesterday's
Session, the saltwater drying and creating a medium
Of bondage between similar elements. Which
Makes me think—why do people spend so much
Energy to be unique when everything's already said?
What's the whole point of it? Why is it a virtue
To express one's feelings and yet no one—
No one—can decipher or understand them?
What is the fucking purpose of it all? Now,
One can grow molehills and one can forge
A journey to the turmeric jungles where
The so-called appointed race can be
Appreciated more than it is already
Appreciated. But what's the purpose
To create this artificial fulfillment
When what's so-called created is false?

Look at those sets, lining up, building peaks

And foaming at the lips then curling into themselves,

On and on, they seem not to end, though

By day's fall I won't be here to see them

Disappear or grow with another intensity. But

Thinking about what Cage said

Intervals between sounds are just important

As the notes themselves, that a melody is comprised

Of tones and atones and silences that are

Bridges that keep everything together.

I wonder if we should pay more attention

Or at least give more credence

To the lull between waves.

92

It's once in a wave bursting over black rocks
That a moment is captured, somewhere
Between telling and feeling. It's a glimpse
That will always stay in memory,
That drop in the wave when the world passes
Right under you, when that liquid tunnel
Compresses you, and all you can see is
The blue rush deafening away all time
And colors that would sparkle your eyes.
You may have been taken to the hairy lips
Or to another endless second over the reef
Or down, never to let you return—oh yes,
How sobering that last one. The fact
It let you remain breathing
So you can write a song is a wonder.

It's broad daylight and the crabs are out to eat,

To scavenge the remainders of the feast held

Just yesterday. Too bad. Most people were not there.

And this smell of fresh limu makes it all better

That I wasn't either. Why, I would have been feeling

A bit stood up as an invitation was not presented to me.

But this limu makes it all the better, that's for sure.

I would rather smell this limu than the bad odors

Permeating, fouling the air and land,

Given off by offals in business suits.

Dull afternoon, with granola bar in hand,

Watching the brown slopes of Diamond Head.

How many eyes can search for pleasures

Before the blinding process ends without ceremony?

The cry on the wind colors the day,

Softens the rocks, makes the water more embracing,

And the floating vegetation is inedible

As the paddle skips the water's surface. But

When the wind turns limp and rapturous,

When the evening promises a purpose

To the random basking of weeds,

Maybe then we can turn to darkness

As a temporary haven for the love of

Sky, moon, transcendence.

Today is my last day and first day
To try something new. The blue sea
Is the same, but it now makes me smile
And let's my mind fall to wonder
Of cold weather outside,
To speak of long shadows and salty air,
Filled with the scent of ambergris.
How far do the ideas of space
And untimely rubble wrinkle the float
Of the flying tags called interlude?
Outside sets are shimmering and holding
Form for carving on flat planes of sand.
And they all huddle around me
With the cold wind laughing too.

The night, with its belated shroud, brings an excitement

To a young boy who is brought to this beach to sleep,

To play, to eat, to live this long dateless weekend.

The lights switch on and off, fly to and fro, and

When the whisper of elements marks whereabouts

Of thunder and sound he can only push along in

The safety of darkness like an old blanket

Over his head covering him with the smells of home.

Later, when the dazzling sun breaks through

The clouds of whirling synapses, he rubs his eyes

And breaks a smile and tugs at the corner of the frame

That has enclosed him: and in the wonder that is now,

Not contained in any color or smell, the boy responds

Once, then twice, to the sensory song he hears

That he will not hear again until many years later.

Gary Pak has published six works of fiction, including *Brothers Under a Same Sky* and *Borderless*. He is a professor emeritus of English at the University of Hawai'i at Mānoa. This is his first book of poems.

Made in the USA
Columbia, SC
25 October 2024

44482962R00069